A voice from Hart

A narrative of events at Harper's Ferry; with incidents prior and subsequent to its capture by Captain Brown and his men

Osborne P. Anderson

Alpha Editions

This edition published in 2024

ISBN : 9789362992994

Design and Setting By
Alpha Editions
www.alphaedis.com
Email - info@alphaedis.com

As per information held with us this book is in Public Domain.
This book is a reproduction of an important historical work. Alpha Editions uses the
best technology to reproduce historical work in the same manner it was first
published to preserve its original nature. Any marks or number seen are left
intentionally to preserve its true form.

Contents

PREFACE. ....- 1 -

CHAPTER I. ....- 2 -

CHAPTER II. ....- 4 -

CHAPTER III. ....- 10 -

CHAPTER IV. ....- 14 -

CHAPTER V. ....- 17 -

CHAPTER VI. ....- 20 -

CHAPTER VII. ....- 22 -

CHAPTER VIII. ....- 24 -

CHAPTER IX. ....- 25 -

CHAPTER X. ....- 28 -

CHAPTER XI. ....- 31 -

CHAPTER XII. ....- 33 -

CHAPTER XIII. ....- 37 -

CHAPTER XIV. ....- 38 -

CHAPTER XV. ....- 41 -

CHAPTER XVI. ....- 43 -

CHAPTER XVII. ....- 46 -

CHAPTER XVIII. ....- 47 -

CHAPTER XIX. ....- 49 -

PREFACE.

My sole purpose in publishing the following Narrative is to save from oblivion the facts connected with one of the most important movements of this age, with reference to the overthrow of American slavery. My own personal experience in it, under the orders of Capt. Brown, on the 16th and 17th of October, 1859, as the only man alive who was at Harper's Ferry during the entire time—the unsuccessful groping after these facts, by individuals, impossible to be obtained, except from an actor in the scene—and the conviction that the cause of impartial liberty requires this duty at my hands—alone have been the motives for writing and circulating the little book herewith presented.

I will not, under such circumstances, insult nor burden the intelligent with excuses for defects in composition, nor for the attempt to give the facts. A plain, unadorned, truthful story is wanted, and that by one who knows what he says, who is known to have been at the great encounter, and to have labored in shaping the same. My identity as a member of Capt. Brown's company cannot be questioned, successfully, by any who are bent upon suppressing the truth; neither will it be by any in Canada or the United States familiar with John Brown and his plans, as those know his men personally, or by reputation, who enjoyed his confidence sufficiently to know thoroughly his plans.

The readers of this narrative will therefore keep steadily in view the main point—that they are perusing a story of events which have happened under the eye of the great Captain, or are incidental thereto, and *not* a compendium of the "plans" of Capt. Brown; for as his plans were not consummated, and as their fulfilment is committed to the future, no one to whom they are known will recklessly expose all of them to the public gaze. Much has been given as true that never happened; much has been omitted that should have been made known; many things have been left unsaid, because, up to within a short time, but two could say them; one of them has been offered up, a sacrifice to the Moloch, Slavery; being that other one, I propose to perform the duty, trusting to that portion of the public who love the right for an appreciation of my endeavor.

O. P. A.

CHAPTER I.

THE IDEA AND ITS EXPONENTS—JOHN BROWN ANOTHER MOSES.

The idea underlying the outbreak at Harper's Ferry is not peculiar to that movement, but dates back to a period very far beyond the memory of the "oldest inhabitant," and emanated from a source much superior to the Wises and Hunters, the Buchanans and Masons of to-day. It was the appointed work for life of an ancient patriarch spoken of in Exodus, chap., ii., and who, true to his great commission, failed not to trouble the conscience and to disturb the repose of the Pharaohs of Egypt with that inexorable, "Thus saith the Lord: Let my people go!" until even they were urgent upon the people in its behalf. Coming down through the nations, and regardless of national boundaries or peculiarities, it has been proclaimed and enforced by the patriarch and the warrior of the Old World, by the enfranchised freeman and the humble slave of the New. Its nationality is universal; its language every where understood by the haters of tyranny; and those that accept its mission, every where understand each other. There is an unbroken chain of sentiment and purpose from Moses of the Jews to John Brown of America; from Kossuth, and the liberators of France and Italy, to the untutored Gabriel, and the Denmark Veseys, Nat Turners and Madison Washingtons of the Southern American States. The shaping and expressing of a thought for freedom takes the same consistence with the colored American—whether he be an independent citizen of the Haytian nation, a proscribed but humble nominally free colored man, a patient, toiling, but hopeful slave—as with the proudest or noblest representative of European or American civilization and Christianity. Lafayette, the exponent of French honor and political integrity, and John Brown, foremost among the men of the New World in high moral and religious principle and magnanimous bravery, embrace as brothers of the same mother, in harmony upon the grand mission of liberty; but, while the Frenchman entered the lists in obedience to a desire to aid, and by invitation from the Adamses and Hamiltons, and thus pushed on the political fortunes of those able to help themselves, John Brown, the liberator of Kansas, the projector and commander of the Harper's Ferry expedition, saw in the most degraded slave a man and a brother, whose appeal for his God-ordained rights no one should disregard; in the toddling slave child, a captive whose release is as imperative, and whose prerogative is as weighty, as the most famous in the land. When the Egyptian pressed hard upon the Hebrew, Moses slew him; and when the spirit of slavery invaded the fair Territory of Kansas, causing the Free-State settlers to cry out because of persecution, old John Brown, famous among the men of God for ever, though then but little known to his fellow-men, called together his sons and went over, as did

Abraham, to the unequal contest, but on the side of the oppressed white men of Kansas that were, and the black men that were to be. To-day, Kansas is free, and the verdict of impartial men is, that to John Brown, more than any other man, Kansas owes her present position.

I am not the biographer of John Brown, but I can be indulged in giving here the opinion common among my people of one so eminently worthy of the highest veneration. Close observation of him, during many weeks, and under his orders at his Kennedy-Farm fireside, also, satisfies me that in comparing the noble old man to Moses, and other men of piety and renown, who were chosen by God to his great work, none have been more faithful, none have given a brighter record.

CHAPTER II.

PRELIMINARIES TO INSURRECTION—WHAT MAY BE TOLD AND WHAT NOT—JOHN BROWN'S FIRST VISIT TO CHATHAM—SOME OF THE SECRETS FROM THE "CARPET-BAG."

To go into particulars, and to detail reports current more than a year before the outbreak, among the many in the United States and Canada who had an inkling of some "practical work" to be done by "Osawattomie Brown," when there should be nothing to do in Kansas,—to give facts in that connection, would only forestall future action, without really benefitting the slave, or winning over to that sort of work the anti-slavery men who do not favor physical resistance to slavery. Slaveholders alone might reap benefits; and for one, I shall throw none in their way, by any indiscreet avowals; they already enjoy more than their share; but to a clear understanding of all the facts to be here published, it may be well to say, that preliminary arrangements were made in a number of places,—plans proposed, discussed and decided upon, numbers invited to participate in the movement, and the list of adherents increased. Nine insurrections is the number given by some as the true list of outbreaks since slavery was planted in America; whether correct or not, it is certain that preliminaries to each are unquestionable. Gabriel, Vesey, Nat Turner, all had conference meetings; all had their plans; but they differ from the Harper's Ferry insurrection in the fact that neither leader nor men, in the latter, divulged ours, when in the most trying of situations. Hark and another met Nat Turner in secret places, after the fatigues of a toilsome day were ended; Gabriel promulged his treason in the silence of the dense forest; but John Brown reasoned of liberty and equality in broad daylight, in a modernized building, in conventions with closed doors, in meetings governed by the elaborate regulations laid down by Jefferson, and used as their guides by Congresses and Legislatures; or he made known the weighty theme, and his comprehensive plans resulting from it, by the cosy fireside, at familiar social gatherings of chosen ones, or better, in the carefully arranged junto of earnest, practical men. Vague hints, careful blinds, are Nat Turner's entire make-up to save detection; the telegraph, the post-office, the railway, all were made to aid the new outbreak. By this, it will be seen that Insurrection has its progressive side, and has been elevated by John Brown from the skulking, fearing cabal, when in the hands of a brave but despairing few, to the highly organized, formidable, and to very many, indispensable institution for the security of freedom, when guided by intelligence.

So much as relates to prior movements may safely be said above; but who met—when they met—where they met—how many yet await the propitious moment—upon whom the mantle of John Brown has fallen to lead on the future army—the certain, terribly certain, many who must follow up the work, forgetting not to gather up the blood of the hero and his slain, to the humble bondman there offered—these may not, must not be told! Of the many meetings in various places, before the work commenced, I shall speak just here of the one, the minutes of which were dragged forth by marauding Virginians from the "archives" at Kennedy Farm; not forgetting, however, for their comfort, that the Convention was one of a series at Chatham, some of which were of equally great, if not greater, importance.

The first visit of John Brown to Chatham was in April, 1858. Wherever he went around, although an entire stranger, he made a profound impression upon those who saw or became acquainted with him. Some supposed him to be a staid but modernized Quaker; others, a solid business man, from "somewhere," and without question a philanthropist. His long white beard, thoughtful and reverent brow and physiognomy, his sturdy, measured tread, as he circulated about with hands, as portrayed in the best lithograph, under the pendant coat-skirt of plain brown Tweed, with other garments to match, revived to those honored with his acquaintance and knowing to his history, the memory of a Puritan of the most exalted type.

After some important business, preparatory to the Convention, was finished, Mr. Brown went West, and returned with his men, who had been spending the winter in Iowa. The party, including the old gentleman, numbered twelve,—as brave, intelligent and earnest a company as could have been associated in one party. There were John H. Kagi, Aaron D. Stevens, Owen Brown, Richard Realf, George B. Gill, C. W. Moffitt, Wm. H. Leeman, John E. Cook, Stewart Taylor, Richard Richardson, Charles P. Tidd and J. S. Parsons—all white except Richard Richardson, who was a slave in Missouri until helped to his liberty by Captain Brown. At a meeting held to prepare for the Convention and to examine the Constitution, Dr. M. R. Delany was Chairman, and John H. Kagi and myself were the Secretaries.

When the Convention assembled, the minutes of which were seized by the slaveholding "cravens" at the Farm, and which, as they have been identified, I shall append to this chapter, Mr. Brown unfolded his plans and purpose. He regarded slavery as a state of perpetual war against the slave, and was fully impressed with the idea that himself and his friends had the right to take liberty, and to use arms in defending the same. Being a devout Bible Christian, he sustained his views and shaped his plans in conformity to the Bible; and when setting them forth, he quoted freely from the Scripture to sustain his position. He realized and enforced the doctrine of destroying the tree that bringeth forth corrupt fruit. Slavery was to him the corrupt tree, and the duty of every Christian man was to strike down slavery, and to commit its fragments to the flames. He was listened to with profound attention, his views were adopted, and the men whose names form a part of the minutes

- 5 -

of that in many respects extraordinary meeting, aided yet further in completing the work.

MINUTES OF THE CONVENTION.

CHATHAM, (Canada West,) }
Saturday, May 8, 1858—10, A. M. }

Convention met in pursuance to a call of John Brown and others, and was called to order by Mr. Jackson, on whose motion, Mr. William C. Munroe was chosen President; when, on motion of Mr. Brown, Mr. J. H. Kagi was elected Secretary.

On motion of Mr. Delany, Mr. Brown then proceeded to state the object of the Convention at length, and then to explain the general features of the plan of action in the execution of the project in view by the Convention. Mr. Delany and others spoke in favor of the project and the plan, and both were agreed to by general consent.

Mr. Brown then presented a plan of organization, entitled "Provisional Constitution and Ordinances for the People of the United States," and moved the reading of the same.

Mr. Kinnard objected to the reading until an oath of secrecy was taken by each member of the Convention; whereupon Mr. Delany moved that the following parole of honor be taken by all the members of the Convention— "I solemnly affirm that I will not in any way divulge any of the secrets of this Convention, except to persons entitled to know the same, on the pain of forfeiting the respect and protection of this organization;" which motion was carried.

The President then proceeded to administer the obligation, after which the question was taken on the reading of the plan proposed by Mr. Brown, and the same carried.

The plan was then read by the Secretary, after which, on motion of Mr. Whipple, it was ordered that it be now read by articles for consideration.

The articles from one to forty-five, inclusive, were then read and adopted. On the reading of the forty-sixth, Mr. Reynolds moved to strike out the same. Reynolds spoke in favor, and Brown, Munroe, Owen Brown, Delany, Realf, Kinnard and Kagi against. The question was then taken and lost, there being but one vote in the affirmative. The article was then adopted.

The forty-seventh and forty-eighth articles, with the schedule, were then adopted in the same manner. It was then moved by Mr. Delany that the title and preamble stand as read. Carried.

On motion of Mr. Kagi, the Constitution, as a whole, was then unanimously adopted.

The Convention then, at half-past one o'clock, P. M., adjourned, on motion of Mr. Jackson, till three o'clock.

THREE O'CLOCK, P. M. Journal read and approved.

On motion of Mr. Delany, it was then ordered that those approving of the Constitution as adopted sign the same; whereupon the names of all the members were appended.

After congratulatory remarks by Messrs. Kinnard and Delany, the Convention, on motion of Mr. Whipple, adjourned at three and three-quarters o'clock.

J. H. KAGI, Secretary of the Convention.

The above is a journal of the Provisional Constitutional Convention held at Chatham, Canada West, May 8, 1858, as herein stated.

CHATHAM, (Canada West,) Saturday, May 8, 1858.

SIX, P. M. In accordance with, and obedience to, the provisions of the schedule to the Constitution for the proscribed and oppressed people "of the United States of America," to-day adopted at this place, a Convention was called by the President of the Convention framing that instrument, and met at the above-named hour, for the purpose of electing officers to fill the offices specially established and named by said Constitution.

The Convention was called to order by Mr. M. R. Delany, upon whose nomination, Mr. Wm. C. Munroe was chosen President, and Mr. J. H. Kagi, Secretary.

A Committee, consisting of Messrs. Whipple, Kagi, Bell, Cook and Munroe, was then chosen to select candidates for the various offices to be filled, for the consideration of the Convention.

On reporting progress, and asking leave to sit again, the request was refused, and Committee discharged.

On motion of Mr. Bell, the Convention then went into the election of officers, in the following manner and order:—

Mr. Whipple nominated John Brown for Commander-in-Chief, who, on the seconding of Mr. Delany, was elected by acclamation.

Mr. Realf nominated J. H. Kagi for Secretary of War, who was elected in the same manner.

On motion of Mr. Brown, the Convention then adjourned to 9, A. M., on Monday, the 10th.

MONDAY, May 10, 1858—9, A. M. The proceedings of the Convention on Saturday were read and approved.

The President announced that the business before the Convention was the further election of officers.

Mr. Whipple nominated Thomas M. Kinnard for President. In a speech of some length, Mr. Kinnard declined.

Mr. Anderson nominated J. W. Loguen for the same office. The nomination was afterwards withdrawn, Mr. Loguen not being present, and it being announced that he would not serve if elected.

Mr. Brown then moved to postpone the election of President for the present. Carried.

The Convention then went into the election of members of Congress. Messrs. A. M. Ellsworth and Osborn Anderson were elected.

After which, the Convention went into the election of Secretary of State, to which office Richard Realf was chosen.

Whereupon the Convention adjourned to half-past two, P. M.

2 1-2, P. M. Convention again assembled, and went into a balloting for the election of Treasurer and Secretary of the Treasury. Owen Brown was elected as the former, and George B. Gill as the latter.

The following resolution was then introduced by Mr. Brown, and unanimously passed:—

Resolved, That John Brown, J. H. Kagi, Richard Realf, L. F. Parsons, C. P. Todd, C. Whipple, C. W. Moffit, John E. Cook, Owen Brown, Stewart Taylor, Osborn Anderson, A. M. Ellsworth, Richard Richardson, W. H. Leeman and John Lawrence be and are hereby appointed a Committee to whom is delegated the power of the Convention to fill by election all the offices specially named in the Provisional Constitution which may be vacant after the adjournment of this Convention.

The Convention then adjourned, *sine die*.

J. H. KAGI, *Secretary of the Convention.*

NAMES OF MEMBERS OF THE CONVENTION, WRITTEN BY EACH PERSON.

William Charles Munroe, President of the Convention; G. J. Reynolds, J. C. Grant, A. J. Smith, James M. Jones, George B. Gill, M. F. Bailey, William Lambert, S. Hunton, C. W. Moffit, John J. Jackson, J. Anderson, Alfred Whipple, James M. Buel, W. H. Leeman, Alfred M. Ellsworth, John E. Cook, Stewart Taylor, James W. Purnell, George Aiken, Stephen Dettin, Thomas Hickerson, John Caunel, Robinson Alexander, Richard Realf, Thomas F. Cary, Richard Richardson, L. F. Parsons, Thomas M. Kinnard, M. H. Delany, Robert Vanvanken, Thomas M, Stringer, Charles P. Tidd, John A. Thomas, C. Whipple, I. D. Shadd, Robert Newman, Owen Brown, John Brown, J. H. Harris, Charles Smith, Simon Fislin, Isaac Holler, James Smith, J. H. Kagi, Secretary of the Convention.

CHAPTER III.

THE WORK GOING BRAVELY ON—THOSE COMMISSIONS—JOHN H. KAGI—A LITTLE CLOUD—"JUDAS" FORBES—ETC.

Many affect to despise the Chatham Convention, and the persons who there abetted the "treason." Governor Wise would like nothing better than to engage the Canadas, with but ten men under his command. By that it is clear that the men acquainted with Brown's plans would not be a "breakfast-spell" for the chivalrous Virginian. In one respect, they were not formidable, and their Constitution would seem to be a harmless paper. Some of them were outlaws against Buchanan Democratic rule in the Territories; some were colored men who had felt severely the proscriptive spirit of American caste; others were escaped slaves, who had left dear kindred behind, writhing in the bloody grasp of the vile man-stealer, never, never to be released, until some practical, daring, determined step should be taken by their friends or their escaped brethren. What use could such men make of a Constitution? Destitute of political or social power, as respects the American States and people, what ghost of an echo could they invoke, by declamation or action, against the peculiar institution? In the light of slaveholding logic and its conclusions, they were but renegade whites and insolent blacks; but, aggregating their grievances, summing up their deep-seated hostility to a system to which every precept of morality, every tie of relationship, is a perpetual protest, the men in Convention, and the many who could not conveniently attend at the time, were not a handful to be despised. The braggadocio of the Virginia Governor might be eager to engage them with ten slaveholders, but John Brown was satisfied with them, and that is honor enough for a generation.

After the Convention adjourned, other business was despatched with utmost speed, and every one seemed in good spirits. The "boys" of the party of "Surveyors," as they were called, were the admired of those who knew them, and the subject of curious remark and inquiry by strangers. So many intellectual looking men are seldom seen in one party, and at the same time, such utter disregard of prevailing custom, or style, in dress and other little conventionalities. Hour after hour they would sit in council, thoughtful, ready; some of them eloquent, all fearless, patient of the fatigues of business; anon, here and there over the "track," and again in the assembly; when the time for relaxation came, sallying forth arm in arm, unshaven, unshorn, and altogether indifferent about it; or one, it may be, impressed with the coming responsibility, sauntering alone, in earnest thought, apparently indifferent to all outward objects, but ready at a word or sign from the chief to undertake any task.

During the sojourn at Chatham, the commissions to the men were discussed, &c. It has been a matter of inquiry, even among friends, why colored men were not commissioned by John Brown to act as captains, lieutenants, &c. I reply, with the knowledge that men in the movement now living will confirm it, that John Brown did offer the captaincy, and other military positions, to colored men equally with others, but a want of acquaintance with military tactics was the invariable excuse. Holding a civil position, as we termed it, I declined a captain's commission tendered by the brave old man, as better suited to those more experienced; and as I was willing to give my life to the cause, trusting to experience and fidelity to make me more worthy, my excuse was accepted. The same must be said of other colored men to be spoken of hereafter, and who proved their worthiness by their able defence of freedom at the Ferry.

JOHN H. KAGI.

Of the constellation of noble men who came to Chatham with Capt. Brown, no one was greater in the essentials of true nobility of character and executive skill than John H. Kagi, the confidential friend and adviser of the old man, and second in position in the expedition; no one was held in more deserved respect. Kagi was, singularly enough, a Virginian by birth, and had relatives in the region of the Ferry. He left home when a youth, an enemy to slavery, and brought as his gift offering to freedom three slaves, whom he piloted to the North. His innate hatred of the institution made him a willing exile from the State of his birth, and his great abilities, natural and acquired, entitled him to the position he held in Capt. Brown's confidence.

Kagi was indifferent to personal appearance; he often went about with slouched hat, one leg of his pantaloons properly adjusted, and the other partly tucked into his high boot-top; unbrushed, unshaven, and in utter disregard of "the latest style"; but to his companions and acquaintances, a verification of Burns' man in the clothes; for John Henry Kagi had improved his time; he discoursed elegantly and fluently, wrote ably, and could occupy the platform with greater ability than many a man known to the American people as famous in these respects. John Brown appreciated him, and to his men, his estimate of John Henry was a familiar theme.

Kagi's bravery, his devotion to the cause, his deference to the commands of his leader, were most nobly illustrated in his conduct at Harper's Ferry.

Scarcely had the Convention and other meetings and business at Chatham been concluded, and most necessary work been done, both at St. Catherines and at this point, when the startling intelligence that the plans were exposed came to hand, and that "Judas" Forbes, after having disclosed some of our important arrangements in the Middle States, was on his way to Washington on a similar errand. This news caused an entire change in the programme for a time. The old gentleman went one way, the young men another, but ultimately to meet in Kansas, in part, where the summer was spent. In the winter of that year, Capt. Brown, J. H. Kagi, A. D. Stevens, C. P. Tidd and Owen Brown, went into Missouri, and released a company of slaves, whom they eventually escorted to Canada, where they are now living and taking care of themselves. An incident of that slave rescue may serve to illustrate more fully the spirit pervading the old man and his "boys." After leaving Missouri with the fugitives, and while yet pursuing the perilous hegira, birth was given to a male child by one of the slave mothers. Dr. Doy, of Kansas, aided in the accouchement, and walked five miles afterwards to get new milk for the boy, while the old Captain named him John Brown, after himself, which name he now bears. At that time, a reward from the United States government was upon the head of Brown; United States Marshals were whisking about, pretendedly eager to arrest them; the weather was very cold, and dangers were upon every hand; but not one jot of comfort or attention for the tender babe and its invalid mother was abated. No thought for their valuable selves, but only how best might the poor and despised charge in their keeping be prudently but really nursed and guarded in their trial journey for liberty. Noble leader of a noble company of men! Yes, reader, whether at Harper's Ferry, or paving the way thither with such deeds as the one here told, and well known West, the old hero and that company were philanthropists to the core. I do not know if the wicked scheme of Forbes may not be excused a little, solely because it afforded the occasion for the great enterprise, growing out of this last visit to Kansas; but Forbes himself must nevertheless be held guilty for its inception, as only ambition to usurp power, and his great love of pelf, (peculiar to him, of all connected with Capt. Brown,) made him dissatisfied, and determined to add falsehood to his other sins against John Brown.

"JUDAS" FORBES.

This Forbes, who, though pretending to disclose some dangerous hornet's nest, was careful enough of his worthless self to tell next to nothing, but to resort to lies, rather from a clear understanding of the consequences, if caught, is an Englishman. When information came, it was not known how much he had told or how little; therefore Brown's precaution to proceed West. From the spring of '58 to the autumn of '59, getting no intelligence of him, it was said he had left America; but instead of that, he lurked around in disguise, feeling, no doubt, that he deserved the punishment of death. Before his defection, he entered into agreement with Capt. Brown to work in the cause of emancipation upon the same terms as did the others, as I repeatedly learned from Brown and his associates, who were acquainted with the matter, and whose veracity stands infinitely above Forbes' word. From Brown, Kagi and Stevens, I learned that the position of second in the organization under the Captain was to be held by "Judas," because of his acquaintance with military science. He was to be drill-master of the company, but not to receive one particle of salary more than the youngest man in the company. But having once gained a secure foothold, he sought to carry out his evil design to make money out of philanthropy, or destroy the movement for ever, could he not be well paid to remain quiet. Money was his object from the first, though disguised; and when he failed to secure that, he raised the question of leadership with Capt. Brown, and that was his excuse for withdrawing from the movement. His heart was clearly never right; but he only delayed, he did not stop the work. When the outbreak occurred, he figured for a little while, though very cautiously, and finally fled to Europe, another Cain, whose mark is unmistakable, and who had better never been born than attempt to stand up among the men he so greatly wronged.

CHAPTER IV.

THE WAY CLEAR—ACTIVE PREPARATIONS—KENNEDY FARM—EMIGRANTS FOR THE SOUTH—CORRESPONDENCE—THE AGENT.

Throughout the summer of 1859, when every thing wore the appearance of perfect quiet, when suspicions were all lulled, when those not fully initiated thought the whole scheme was abandoned, arrangements were in active preparation for the work. Mr. Brown, Kagi, and a part of the Harper's Ferry company, who had previously spent some time in Ohio, went into Pennsylvania in the month of June, and up to the early part of July, having made necessary observations, they penetrated the Keystone yet further, and laid plans to receive freight and men as they should arrive. Under the assumed name of Smith, Captain Brown pushed his explorations further south, and selected

KENNEDY FARM.

Kennedy Farm, in every respect an excellent location for *business* as "head-quarters," was rented at a cheap rate, and men and freight were sent thither. Capt. Brown returned to ——, and sent freight, while Kagi was stationed at ——, to correspond with persons elsewhere, and to receive and despatch freight as it came. Owen, Watson, and Oliver Brown, took their position at head-quarters, to receive whatever was sent. These completed the arrangements. The Captain labored and travelled night and day, sometimes on old Dolly, his brown mule, and sometimes in the wagon. He would start directly after night, and travel the fifty miles between the Farm and Chambersburg by daylight next morning; and he otherwise kept open communication between head-quarters and the latter place, in order that matters might be arranged in due season.

John H. Kagi wrote for freight, and the following letter, before published in relation to it, was written by a co-laborer:

WEST ANDOVER, Ohio, July 30th, 1859.

JOHN HENRIE, Esq.:

DEAR SIR,—I yesterday received yours of the 25th inst., together with letter of instructions from our mutual friend Isaac, enclosing draft for $100. Have written you as many as three letters, I think, before this, and have received all you have sent, probably.

The heavy freight of fifteen boxes I sent off some days ago. The household stuff, consisting of six boxes and one chest, I have put in good shape, and shall, I think, be able to get them on their way on Monday next, and shall myself be on my way northward within a day or two after.

Enclosed please find list of contents of boxes, which it may be well to preserve.

The freight having arrived in good condition, John Henrie replies.

As the Kennedy Farm is a part of history, a slight allusion to its location may not be out of place, although it has been so frequently spoken of as to be almost universally known. The Farm is located in Washington County, Maryland, in a mountainous region, on the road from Chambersburg; it is in a comparatively non-slaveholding population, four miles from Harper's Ferry. Yet, among the few traders in the souls of men located around, several circumstances peculiar to the institution happened while the party sojourned there, which serve to show up its hideous character. During three weeks of my residence at the Farm, no less than four deaths took place among the slaves; one, Jerry, living three miles away, hung himself in the late Dr. Kennedy's orchard, because he was to be sold South, his master having become insolvent. The other three cases were homicides; they were punished so that death ensued immediately, or in a short time. It was the knowledge of these atrocities, and the melancholy suicide named, that caused Oliver Brown, when writing to his young wife, to refer directly to the deplorable aspect of slavery in that neighborhood. Once fairly established, and freight having arrived safely, the published correspondence becomes significant to an actor in the scene. Emigrants began to drop down, from this quarter and the other. Smith writes to Kagi:—

WEST ANDOVER, Ashtabula Co., O., Wednesday, 1859.

FRIEND HENRIE,—Yours of the 14th inst. I received last night—glad to learn that the "Wire" has arrived in good condition, and that our "R" friend was pleased with a view of those "pre-eventful shadows."

Shall write Leary at once, also our other friends at the North and East. Am highly pleased with the prospect I have of doing something to the purpose now, right away, here and in contiguous sections, in the way of getting stock taken. I am devoting my whole time to our work. Write often, and keep me posted up close. [Here follow some phonographic characters, which may be read: "I have learned phonography, but not enough to correspond to any advantage. Can probably read any thing you may write, if written in the corresponding style."]

Faithfully yours,
JOHN SMITH.

Please say to father to address [phonographic characters which might read "John Luther"] when he writes me. I wish you to see what I have written him.

J. S.

THE AGENT.

In the month of August, 1859, John Brown's Agent spent some time in Canada. He visited Chatham, Buxton, and other places, and formed Liberty Leagues, and arranged matters so that operations could be carried on with excellent success, through the efficiency of Messrs. C., S., B., and L., the Chairman, Corresponding Secretary, Secretary O., and Treasurer of the Society. He then proceeded to Detroit, where another Society is established. So well satisfied was Captain Brown with the work done, that he wrote in different directions: "The fields whiten unto harvest;" and again, "Your friends at head-quarters want you at their elbow." This was an invitation by the good old man to as brave and efficient a laborer in the cause of human rights as the friends of freedom have ever known; and to one who must yet bear the beacon-light of liberty before the self-emancipated bondmen of the South.

CHAPTER V.

MORE CORRESPONDENCE—MY JOURNEY TO THE FERRY—A GLANCE AT THE FAMILY.

Preparations had so far progressed, up to the time when incidents mentioned in the preceding chapter had taken place, that Kagi wrote to Chatham and other places, urging parties favorable to come on without loss of time. In reply to the letter written to Chatham, soliciting volunteers, the appended, from an office-bearer, referred to my own journey to the South:—

DEAR SIR,—Yours came to hand last night. One hand (Anderson) left here last night, and will be found an efficient hand. Richardson is anxious to be at work as a missionary to bring sinners to repentance. He will start in a few days. Another will follow immediately after, if not with him. More laborers may be looked for shortly. "Slow but sure."

Alexander has received yours, so you see all communications have come to hand, so far. Alexander is not coming up to the work as he agreed. I fear he will be found unreliable in the end.

Dull times affect missionary matters here more than any thing else; however, a few active laborers may be looked for as certain.

I would like to hear of your congregation numbering more than "15 and 2" to commence a good revival; still, our few will be adding strength to the good work.

Yours, &c.,
J. M. B.

To J. B., Jr.

As set forth in this letter, I left Canada September 13th, and reached ——, in Pennsylvania, three days after. On my arrival, I was surprised to learn that the freight was all moved to head-quarters, but a few boxes, the arrival of which, the evening of the same day, called forth from Kagi the following brief note:—

CHAMBERSBURG, ——, ——

J. SMITH & SONS,—A quantity of freight has to-day arrived for you in care of Oaks & Caufman. The amount is somewhere between 2,600 and 3,000 lbs. Charges in full, $25.98. The character is, according to manifest, 33 bundles and 4 boxes.

I yesterday received a letter from John Smith, containing nothing of any particular importance, however, so I will keep it until you come up.

Respectfully,
J. HENRIE.

CHAMBERSBURG, Pa., Friday, Sept. 16, 1859, }
11 o'clock, A. M. }

J. SMITH AND SONS,—I have just time to say that Mr. Anderson arrived in the train five minutes ago.

Respectfully,
J. HENRIE.

P. S. I have not had time to talk with him.

J. H.

A little while prior to this, * * went down to ——, to accompany Shields Green, whereupon a meeting of Capt. Brown, Kagi, and other distinguished persons, convened for consultation.

On the 20th, four days after I reached this outpost, Capt. Brown, Watson Brown, Kagi, myself, and several friends, held another meeting, after which, on the 24th, I left Chambersburg for Kennedy Farm. I walked alone as far as Middletown, a town on the line between Maryland and Pennsylvania, and it being then dark, I found Captain Brown awaiting with his wagon. We set out directly, and drove until nearly day-break the next morning, when we reached the Farm in safety. As a very necessary precaution against surprise, all the colored men at the Ferry who went from the North, made the journey from the Pennsylvania line in the night. I found all the men concerned in the undertaking on hand when I arrived, excepting Copeland, Leary, and Merriam; and when all had collected, a more earnest, fearless, determined company of men it would be difficult to get together. There, as at Chatham, I saw the same evidence of strong and commanding intellect, high-toned morality, and inflexibility of purpose in the men, and a profound and holy reverence for God, united to the most comprehensive, practical, systematic philanthropy, and undoubted bravery in the patriarch leader, brought out to view in lofty grandeur by the associations and surroundings of the place and the occasion. There was no milk and water sentimentality—no offensive contempt for the negro, while working in his cause; the pulsations of each and every heart beat in harmony for the suffering and pleading slave. I thank God that I have been permitted to realize to its furthest, fullest extent, the moral, mental, physical, social harmony of an Anti-Slavery family, carrying out to the letter the principles of its antetype, the Anti-Slavery cause. In John Brown's house, and in John Brown's presence, men from widely different parts of the continent met and united into one company, wherein no hateful prejudice dared intrude its ugly self—no ghost of a distinction found space to enter.

CHAPTER VI.

LIFE AT KENNEDY FARM.

To a passer-by, the house and its surroundings presented but indifferent attractions. Any log tenement of equal dimensions would be as likely to arrest a stray glance. Rough, unsightly, and aged, it was only those privileged to enter and tarry for a long time, and to penetrate the mysteries of the two rooms it contained—kitchen, parlor, dining-room below, and the spacious chamber, attic, store-room, prison, drilling room, comprised in the loft above—who could tell how we lived at Kennedy Farm.

Every morning, when the noble old man was at home, he called the family around, read from his Bible, and offered to God most fervent and touching supplications for all flesh; and especially pathetic were his petitions in behalf of the oppressed. I never heard John Brown pray, that he did not make strong appeals to God for the deliverance of the slave. This duty over, the men went to the loft, there to remain all the day long; few only could be seen about, as the neighbors were watchful and suspicious. It was also important to talk but little among ourselves, as visitors to the house might be curious. Besides the daughter and daughter-in-law, who superintended the work, some one or other of the men was regularly detailed to assist in the cooking, washing, and other domestic work. After the ladies left, we did all the work, no one being exempt, because of age or official grade in the organization.

The principal employment of the prisoners, as we severally were when compelled to stay in the loft, was to study Forbes' Manual, and to go through a quiet, though rigid drill, under the training of Capt. Stevens, at some times. At others, we applied a preparation for bronzing our gun barrels—discussed subjects of reform—related our personal history; but when our resources became pretty well exhausted, the *ennui* from confinement, imposed silence, etc., would make the men almost desperate. At such times, neither slavery nor slaveholders were discussed mincingly. We were, while the ladies remained, often relieved of much of the dullness growing out of restraint by their kindness. As we could not circulate freely, they would bring in wild fruit and flowers from the woods and fields. We were well supplied with grapes, paw-paws, chestnuts, and other small fruit, besides bouquets of fall flowers, through their thoughtful consideration.

During the several weeks I remained at the encampment, we were under the restraint I write of through the day; but at night, we sallied out for a ramble, or to breathe the fresh air and enjoy the beautiful solitude of the mountain scenery around, by moonlight.

Captain Brown loved the fullest expression of opinion from his men, and not seldom, when a subject was being severely scrutinized by Kagi, Oliver, or others of the party, the old gentleman would be one of the most interested and earnest hearers. Frequently his views were severely criticised, when no one would be in better spirits than himself. He often remarked that it was gratifying to see young men grapple with moral and other important questions, and express themselves independently; it was evidence of self-sustaining power.

CHAPTER VII.

CAPTAIN BROWN AND J. H. KAGI GO TO PHILADELPHIA— F. J. MERRIAM, J. COPELAND AND S. LEARY ARRIVE— MATTERS PRECIPITATED BY INDISCRETION.

Being obliged, from the space I propose to give to this narrative, to omit many incidents of my sojourn at the Farm, which from association are among my most pleasant recollections, the events now to be recorded are to me invested with the most intense interest. About ten days before the capture of the Ferry, Captain John Brown and Kagi went to Philadelphia, on business of great importance. How important, men there and elsewhere *now* know. How affected by, and affecting the main features of the enterprise, we at the Farm knew full well after their return, as the old Captain, in the fullness of his overflowing, saddened heart, detailed point after point of interest. God bless the old veteran, who could and did chase a thousand in life, and defied more than ten thousand by the moral sublimity of his death!

On their way home, at Chambersburg, they met young F. J. Merriam, of Boston. Several days were spent at C., when Merriam left for Baltimore, to purchase some necessary articles for the undertaking. John Copeland and Sherrard Lewis Leary reached Chambersburg on the 12th of October, and on Saturday, the 15th, at daylight, they arrived, in company with Kagi and Watson Brown. In the evening of the same day, F. J. Merriam came to the Farm.

Saturday, the 15th, was a busy day for all hands. The chief and every man worked busily, packing up, and getting ready to remove the means of defence to the school-house, and for further security, as the people living around were in a state of excitement, from having seen a number of men about the premises a few days previously. Not being fully satisfied as to the real business of "J. Smith & Sons" after that, and learning that several thousand stand of arms were to be removed by the Government from the Armory to some other point, threats to search the premises were made against the encampment. A tried friend having given information of the state of public feeling without, and of the intended process, Captain Brown and party concluded to strike the blow immediately, and not, as at first intended, to await certain reinforcements from the North and East, which would have been in Maryland within one and three weeks. Could other parties, waiting for the word, have reached head-quarters in time for the outbreak when it took place, the taking of the armory, engine house, and rifle factory, would have been quite different. But the men at the Farm had been so closely confined, that they went out about the house and farm in the day-time during that week, and so indiscreetly exposed their numbers to the prying neighbors, who thereupon took steps to have a search instituted in the early part of the coming week. Capt. Brown was not seconded in another quarter as he expected at the time of the action, but could the fears of the neighbors have been allayed for a few days, the disappointment in the former respect would not have had much weight.

The indiscretion alluded to has been greatly lamented by all of us, as Maryland, Virginia, and other slave States, had, as they now have, a direct interest in the successful issue of the first step. Few ultimately successful movements were predicated on the issue of the first bold stroke, and so it is with the institution of slavery. It will yet come down by the run, but it will not be because huzzas of victory were shouted over the first attempt, any more than at Bunker Hill or Hastings.

CHAPTER VIII.

COUNCIL MEETINGS—ORDERS GIVEN—THE CHARGE—ETC.

On Sunday morning, October 16th, Captain Brown arose earlier than usual, and called his men down to worship. He read a chapter from the Bible, applicable to the condition of the slaves, and our duty as their brethren, and then offered up a fervent prayer to God to assist in the liberation of the bondmen in that slaveholding land. The services were impressive beyond expression. Every man there assembled seemed to respond from the depths of his soul, and throughout the entire day, a deep solemnity pervaded the place. The old man's usually weighty words were invested with more than ordinary importance, and the countenance of every man reflected the momentous thought that absorbed his attention within.

After breakfast had been despatched, and the roll called by the Captain, a sentinel was posted outside the door, to warn by signal if any one should approach, and we listened to preparatory remarks to a council meeting to be held that day. At 10 o'clock, the council was assembled. I was appointed to the Chair, when matters of importance were considered at length. After the council adjourned, the Constitution was read for the benefit of the few who had not before heard it, and the necessary oaths taken. Men who were to hold military positions in the organization, and who had not received commissions before then, had their commissions filled out by J. H. Kagi, and gave the required obligations.

In the afternoon, the eleven orders presented in the next chapter were given by the Captain, and were afterwards carried out in every particular by the officers and men.

In the evening, before setting out to the Ferry, he gave his final charge, in which he said, among other things:—*"And now, gentlemen, let me impress this one thing upon your minds. You all know how dear life is to you, and how dear your life is to your friends. And in remembering that, consider that the lives of others are as dear to them as yours are to you. Do not, therefore, take the life of any one, if you can possibly avoid it; but if it is necessary to take life in order to save your own, then make sure work of it."*

CHAPTER IX.

THE ELEVEN ORDERS GIVEN BY CAPTAIN BROWN TO HIS MEN BEFORE SETTING OUT FOR THE FERRY.

The orders given by Captain Brown, before departing from the Farm for the Ferry, were:—

1. Captain Owen Brown, F. J. Merriam, and Barclay Coppic to remain at the old house as sentinels, to guard the arms and effects till morning, when they would be joined by some of the men from the Ferry with teams to move all arms and other things to the old school-house before referred to, located about three-quarters of a mile from Harper's Ferry—a place selected a day or two beforehand by the Captain.

2. All hands to make as little noise as possible going to the Ferry, so as not to attract attention till we could get to the bridge; and to keep all arms secreted, so as not to be detected if met by any one.

3. The men were to walk in couples, at some distance apart; and should any one overtake us, stop him and detain him until the rest of our comrades were out of the road. The same course to be pursued if we were met by any one.

4. That Captains Charles P. Tidd and John E. Cook walk ahead of the wagon in which Captain Brown rode to the Ferry, to tear down the telegraph wires on the Maryland side along the railroad; and to do the same on the Virginia side, after the town should be captured.

5. Captains John H. Kagi and A. D. Stevens were to take the watchman at the Ferry bridge prisoner when the party got there, and to detain him there until the engine house upon the Government grounds should be taken.

6. Captain Watson Brown and Stewart Taylor were to take positions at the Potomac bridge, and hold it till morning. They were to stand on opposite sides, a rod apart, and if any one entered the bridge, they were to let him get in between them. In that case, pikes were to be used, not Sharp's rifles, unless they offered much resistance, and refused to surrender.

7. Captains Oliver Brown and William Thompson were to execute a similar order at the Shenandoah bridge, until morning.

8. Lieutenant Jeremiah Anderson and Adolphus Thompson were to occupy the engine house at first, with the prisoner watchman from the bridge and the watchman belonging to the engine-house yard, until the one on the opposite side of the street and the rifle factory were taken, after which they would be reinforced, to hold that place with the prisoners.

9. Lieutenant Albert Hazlett and Private Edwin Coppic were to hold the Armory opposite the engine house after it had been taken, through the night and until morning, when arrangements would be different.

10. That John H. Kagi, Adjutant General, and John A. Copeland, (colored,) take positions at the rifle factory through the night, and hold it until further orders.

11. That Colonel A. D. Stevens (the same Captain Stevens who held military position next to Captain Brown) proceed to the country with his men, and after taking certain parties prisoners bring them to the Ferry. In the case of Colonel Lewis Washington, who had arms in his hands, he must, before being secured as a prisoner, deliver them into the hands of Osborne P. Anderson. Anderson being a colored man, and colored men being only *things* in the South, it is proper that the South be taught a lesson upon this point.

John H. Kagi being Adjutant General, was the near adviser of Captain John Brown, and second in position; and had the old gentleman been slain at the Ferry, and Kagi been spared, the command would have devolved upon the latter. But Col. Stevens holding the active military position in the organization second to Captain Brown, when order eleven was given him, had the privilege of choosing his own men to execute it. The selection was made after the capture of the Ferry, and then my duty to receive Colonel Washington's famous arms was assigned me by Captain Brown. The men selected by Col. Stevens to act under his orders during the night were Charles P. Tidd, Osborne P. Anderson, Shields Green, John E. Cook, and Sherrard Lewis Leary. We were to take prisoners, and any slaves who would come, and bring them to the Ferry.

A few days before, Capt. Cook had travelled along the Charlestown turnpike, and collected statistics of the population of slaves and the masters' names. Among the masters whose acquaintance Cook had made, Colonel Washington had received him politely, and had shown him a sword formerly owned by Frederic the Great of Prussia, and presented by him to Genl. Washington, and a pair of horse pistols, formerly owned by General Lafayette, and bequeathed by the old General to Lewis Washington. These were the arms specially referred to in the charge.

At eight o'clock on Sunday evening, Captain Brown said: "Men, get on your arms; we will proceed to the Ferry." His horse and wagon were brought out before the door, and some pikes, a sledge-hammer and crowbar were placed in it. The Captain then put on his old Kansas cap, and said: "Come, boys!" when we marched out of the camp behind him, into the lane leading down the hill to the main road. As we formed the procession line, Owen Brown, Barclay Coppic, and Francis J. Merriam, sentinels left behind to protect the place as before stated, came forward and took leave of us; after which, agreeably to previous orders, and as they were better acquainted with the topography of the Ferry, and to effect the tearing down of the telegraph wires, C. P. Tidd and John E. Cook led the procession. While going to the Ferry, the company marched along as solemnly as a funeral procession, till we got to the bridge. When we entered, we halted, and carried out an order to fasten our cartridge boxes outside of our clothes, when every thing was ready for taking the town.

CHAPTER X.

THE CAPTURE OF HARPER'S FERRY—COL. A. D. STEVENS AND PARTY SALLY OUT TO THE PLANTATIONS—WHAT WE SAW, HEARD, DID, ETC.

As John H. Kagi and A. D. Stevens entered the bridge, as ordered in the fifth charge, the watchman, being at the other end, came toward them with a lantern in his hand. When up to them, they told him he was their prisoner, and detained him a few minutes, when he asked them to spare his life. They replied, they did not intend to harm him; the object was to free the slaves, and he would have to submit to them for a time, in order that the purpose might be carried out.

Captain Brown now entered the bridge in his wagon, followed by the rest of us, until we reached that part where Kagi and Stevens held their prisoner, when he ordered Watson Brown and Stewart Taylor to take the positions assigned them in order sixth, and the rest of us to proceed to the engine house. We started for the engine house, taking the prisoner along with us. When we neared the gates of the engine-house yard, we found them locked, and the watchman on the inside. He was told to open the gates, but refused, and commenced to cry. The men were then ordered by Captain Brown to open the gates forcibly, which was done, and the watchman taken prisoner. The two prisoners were left in the custody of Jerry Anderson and Adolphus Thompson, and A. D. Stevens arranged the men to take possession of the Armory and rifle factory. About this time, there was apparently much excitement. People were passing back and forth in the town, and before we could do much, we had to take several prisoners. After the prisoners were secured, we passed to the opposite side of the street and took the Armory, and Albert Hazlett and Edwin Coppic were ordered to hold it for the time being.

The capture of the rifle factory was the next work to be done. When we went there, we told the watchman who was outside of the building our business, and asked him to go along with us, as we had come to take possession of the town, and make use of the Armory in carrying out our object. He obeyed the command without hesitation. John H. Kagi and John Copeland were placed in the Armory, and the prisoners taken to the engine house. Following the capture of the Armory, Oliver Brown and William Thompson were ordered to take possession of the bridge leading out of town, across the Shenandoah river, which they immediately did. These places were all taken, and the prisoners secured, without the snap of a gun, or any violence whatever.

The town being taken, Brown, Stevens, and the men who had no post in charge, returned to the engine house, where council was held, after which

Captain Stevens, Tidd, Cook, Shields Green, Leary and myself went to the country. On the road, we met some colored men, to whom we made known our purpose, when they immediately agreed to join us. They said they had been long waiting for an opportunity of the kind. Stevens then asked them to go around among the colored people and circulate the news, when each started off in a different direction. The result was that many colored men gathered to the scene of action. The first prisoner taken by us was Colonel Lewis Washington. When we neared his house, Capt. Stevens placed Leary and Shields Green to guard the approaches to the house, the one at the side, the other in front. We then knocked, but no one answering, although females were looking from upper windows, we entered the building and commenced a search for the proprietor. Col. Washington opened his room door, and begged us not to kill him. Capt. Stevens replied, "You are our prisoner," when he stood as if speechless or petrified. Stevens further told him to get ready to go to the Ferry; that he had come to abolish slavery, not to take life but in self-defence, but that he *must* go along. The Colonel replied: "You can have my slaves, if you will let me remain." "No," said the Captain, "you must go along too; so get ready." After saying this, Stevens left the house for a time, and with Green, Leary and Tidd, proceeded to the "Quarters," giving the prisoner in charge of Cook and myself. The male slaves were gathered together in a short time, when horses were tackled to the Colonel's two-horse carriage and four-horse wagon, and both vehicles brought to the front of the house.

During this time, Washington was walking the floor, apparently much excited. When the Captain came in, he went to the sideboard, took out his whiskey, and offered us something to drink, but he was refused. His fire-arms were next demanded, when he brought forth one double-barrelled gun, one small rifle, two horse-pistols and a sword. Nothing else was asked of him. The Colonel cried heartily when he found he must submit, and appeared taken aback when, on delivering up the famous sword formerly presented by Frederic to his illustrious kinsman, George Washington, Capt. Stevens told me to step forward and take it. Washington was secured and placed in his wagon, the women of the family making great outcries, when the party drove forward to Mr. John Allstadt's. After making known our business to him, he went into as great a fever of excitement as Washington had done. We could have his slaves, also, if we would only leave him. This, of course, was contrary to our plans and instructions. He hesitated, puttered around, fumbled and meditated for a long time. At last, seeing no alternative, he got ready, when the slaves were gathered up from about the quarters by their own consent, and all placed in Washington's big wagon and returned to the Ferry.

One old colored lady, at whose house we stopped, a little way from the town, had a good time over the message we took her. This liberating the slaves was the very thing she had longed for, prayed for, and dreamed about, time and again; and her heart was full of rejoicing over the fulfilment of a prophecy which had been her faith for long years. While we were absent from the Ferry, the train of cars for Baltimore arrived, and was detained. A colored man named Haywood, employed upon it, went from the Wager House up to the entrance to the bridge, where the train stood, to assist with the baggage. He was ordered to stop by the sentinels stationed at the bridge, which he refused to do, but turned to go in an opposite direction, when he was fired upon, and received a mortal wound. Had he stood when ordered, he would not have been harmed. No one knew at the time whether he was white or colored, but his movements were such as to justify the sentinels in shooting him, as he would not stop when commanded. The first firing happened at that time, and the only firing, until after daylight on Monday morning.

CHAPTER XI.

THE EVENTS OF MONDAY, OCT. 17—ARMING THE SLAVES—TERROR IN THE SLAVEHOLDING CAMP—IMPORTANT LOSSES TO OUR PARTY—THE FATE OF KAGI—PRISONERS ACCUMULATE—WORKMEN AT THE KENNEDY FARM—ETC.

Monday, the 17th of October, was a time of stirring and exciting events. In consequence of the movements of the night before, we were prepared for commotion and tumult, but certainly not for more than we beheld around us. Gray dawn and yet brighter daylight revealed great confusion, and as the sun arose, the panic spread like wild-fire. Men, women and children could be seen leaving their homes in every direction; some seeking refuge among residents, and in quarters further away, others climbing up the hill-sides, and hurrying off in various directions, evidently impelled by a sudden fear, which was plainly visible in their countenances or in their movements.

Capt. Brown was all activity, though I could not help thinking that at times he appeared somewhat puzzled. He ordered Sherrard Lewis Leary, and four slaves, and a free man belonging in the neighborhood, to join John Henry Kagi and John Copeland at the rifle factory, which they immediately did. Kagi, and all except Copeland, were subsequently killed, but not before having communicated with Capt. Brown, as will be set forth further along.

As fast as the workmen came to the building, or persons appeared in the street near the engine house, they were taken prisoners, and directly after sunrise, the detained train was permitted to start for the eastward. After the departure of the train, quietness prevailed for a short time; a number of prisoners were already in the engine house, and of the many colored men living in the neighborhood, who had assembled in the town, a number were armed for the work.

Capt. Brown ordered Capts. Charles P. Tidd, Wm. H. Leeman, John E. Cook, and some fourteen slaves, to take Washington's four-horse wagon, and to join the company under Capt. Owen Brown, consisting of F. J. Merriam and Barclay Coppic, who had been left at the Farm the night previous, to guard the place and the arms. The company, thus reinforced, proceeded, under Owen Brown, to move the arms and goods from the Farm down to the school-house in the mountains, three-fourths of a mile from the Ferry.

Capt. Brown next ordered me to take the pikes out of the wagon in which he rode to the Ferry, and to place them in the hands of the colored men who had come with us from the plantations, and others who had come forward without having had communication with any of our party. It was out of the circumstances connected with the fulfilment of this order, that the false charge against "Anderson" as leader, or "ringleader," of the negroes, grew.

The spectators, about this time, became apparently wild with fright and excitement. The number of prisoners was magnified to hundreds, and the judgment-day could not have presented more terrors, in its awful and certain prospective punishment to the justly condemned for the wicked deeds of a life-time, the chief of which would no doubt be slaveholding, than did Capt. Brown's operations.

The prisoners were also terror-stricken. Some wanted to go home to see their families, as if for the last time. The privilege was granted them, under escort, and they were brought back again. Edwin Coppic, one of the sentinels at the Armory gate, was fired at by one of the citizens, but the ball did not reach him, when one of the insurgents close by put up his rifle, and made the enemy bite the dust.

Among the arms taken from Col. Washington was one double-barrel gun. This weapon was loaded by Leeman with buckshot, and placed in the hands of an elderly slave man, early in the morning. After the cowardly charge upon Coppic, this old man was ordered by Capt. Stevens to arrest a citizen. The old man ordered him to halt, which he refused to do, when instantly the terrible load was discharged into him, and he fell, and expired without a struggle.

After these incidents, time passed away till the arrival of the United States troops, without any further attack upon us. The cowardly Virginians submitted like sheep, without resistance, from that time until the marines came down. Meanwhile, Capt. Brown, who was considering a proposition for release from his prisoners, passed back and forth from the Armory to the bridge, speaking words of comfort and encouragement to his men. "Hold on a little longer, boys," said he, "until I get matters arranged with the prisoners." This tardiness on the part of our brave leader was sensibly felt to be an omen of evil by some us, and was eventually the cause of our defeat. It was no part of the original plan to hold on to the Ferry, or to parley with prisoners; but by so doing, time was afforded to carry the news of its capture to several points, and forces were thrown into the place, which surrounded us.

At eleven o'clock, Capt. Brown despatched William Thompson from the Ferry up to Kennedy Farm, with the news that we had peaceful possession of the town, and with directions to the men to continue on moving the things. He went; but before he could get back, troops had begun to pour in, and the general encounter commenced.

CHAPTER XII.

RECEPTION TO THE TROOPS—THEY RETREAT TO THE BRIDGE—A PRISONER—DEATH OF DANGERFIELD NEWBY—WILLIAM THOMPSON—THE MOUNTAINS ALIVE—FLAG OF TRUCE—THE ENGINE HOUSE TAKEN.

It was about twelve o'clock in the day when we were first attacked by the troops. Prior to that, Capt. Brown, in anticipation of further trouble, had girded to his side the famous sword taken from Col. Lewis Washington the night before, and with that memorable weapon, he commanded his men against General Washington's own State.

When the Captain received the news that the troops had entered the bridge from the Maryland side, he, with some of his men, went into the street, and sent a message to the Arsenal for us to come forth also. We hastened to the street as ordered, when he said—"The troops are on the bridge, coming into town; we will give them a warm reception." He then walked around amongst us, giving us words of encouragement, in this wise:—"Men! be cool! Don't waste your powder and shot! Take aim, and make every shot count!" "The troops will look for us to retreat on their first appearance; be careful to shoot first." Our men were well supplied with fire-arms, but Capt. Brown had no rifle at that time; his only weapon was the sword before mentioned.

The troops soon came out of the bridge, and up the street facing us, we occupying an irregular position. When they got within sixty or seventy yards, Capt. Brown said, "Let go upon them!" which we did, when several of them fell. Again and again the dose was repeated.

There was now consternation among the troops. From marching in solid martial columns, they became scattered. Some hastened to seize upon and bear up the wounded and dying,—several lay dead upon the ground. They seemed not to realize, at first, that we would fire upon them, but evidently expected we would be driven out by them without firing. Capt. Brown seemed fully to understand the matter, and hence, very properly and in our defence, undertook to forestall their movements. The consequence of their unexpected reception was, after leaving several of their dead on the field, they beat a confused retreat into the bridge, and there stayed under cover until reinforcements came to the Ferry.

On the retreat of the troops, we were ordered back to our former post. While going, Dangerfield Newby, one of our colored men, was shot through the head by a person who took aim at him from a brick store window, on the opposite side of the street, and who was there for the purpose of firing upon us. Newby was a brave fellow. He was one of my comrades at the Arsenal.

He fell at my side, and his death was promptly avenged by Shields Green, the Zouave of the band, who afterwards met his fate calmly on the gallows, with John Copeland. Newby was shot twice; at the first fire, he fell on his side and returned it; as he lay, a second shot was fired, and the ball entered his head. Green raised his rifle in an instant, and brought down the cowardly murderer, before the latter could get his gun back through the sash.

There was comparative quiet for a time, except that the citizens seemed to be wild with terror. Men, women and children forsook the place in great haste, climbing up hill-sides and scaling the mountains. The latter seemed to be alive with white fugitives, fleeing from their doomed city. During this time, Wm. Thompson, who was returning from his errand to the Kennedy Farm, was surrounded on the bridge by the railroad men, who next came up, taken a prisoner to the Wager House, tied hand and foot, and, at a late hour of the afternoon, cruelly murdered by being riddled with balls, and thrown headlong on the rocks.

Late in the morning, some of his prisoners told Capt. Brown that they would like to have breakfast, when he sent word forthwith to the Wager House to that effect, and they were supplied. He did not order breakfast for himself and men, as was currently but falsely stated at the time, as he suspected foul play; on the contrary, when solicited to have breakfast so provided for him, he refused.

Between two and three o'clock in the afternoon, armed men could be seen coming from every direction; soldiers were marching and counter-marching; and on the mountains, a host of blood-thirsty ruffians swarmed, waiting for their opportunity to pounce upon the little band. The fighting commenced in earnest after the arrival of fresh troops. Volley upon volley was discharged, and the echoes from the hills, the shrieks of the townspeople, and the groans of their wounded and dying, all of which filled the air, were truly frightful. The Virginians may well conceal their losses, and Southern chivalry may hide its brazen head, for their boasted bravery was well tested that day, and in no way to their advantage. It is remarkable, that except that one foolhardy colored man was reported buried, no other funeral is mentioned, although the Mayor and other citizens are known to have fallen. Had they reported the true number, their disgrace would have been more apparent; so they wisely (?) concluded to be silent.

The fight at Harper's Ferry also disproved the current idea that slaveholders will lay down their lives for their property. Col. Washington, the representative of the old hero, stood "blubbering" like a great calf at supposed danger; while the laboring white classes and non-slaveholders, with the marines, (mostly gentlemen from "furrin" parts,) were the men who faced the bullets of John Brown and his men. Hardly the skin of a slaveholder could be scratched in open fight; the cowards kept out of the way until danger was passed, sending the poor whites into the pitfalls, while they were reserved for the bragging, and to do the safe but cowardly judicial murdering afterwards.

As strangers poured in, the enemy took positions round about, so as to prevent any escape, within shooting distance of the engine house and Arsenal. Capt. Brown, seeing their manœuvres, said: "We will hold on to our three positions, if they are unwilling to come to terms, and die like men."

All this time, the fight was progressing; no powder and ball were wasted. We shot from under cover, and took deadly aim. For an hour before the flag of truce was sent out, the firing was uninterrupted, and one and another of the enemy were constantly dropping to the earth.

One of the Captain's plans was to keep up communication between his three points. In carrying out this idea, Jerry Anderson went to the rifle factory, to see Kagi and his men. Kagi, fearing that we would be overpowered by numbers if the Captain delayed leaving, sent word by Anderson to advise him to leave the town at once. This word Anderson communicated to the Captain, and told us also at the Arsenal. The message sent back to Kagi was, to hold out for a few minutes longer, when we would all evacuate the place. Those few minutes proved disastrous, for then it was that the troops before spoken of came pouring in, increased by crowds of men from the surrounding country. After an hour's hard fighting, and when the enemy were blocking up the avenues of escape, Capt. Brown sent out his son Watson with a flag of truce, but no respect was paid to it; he was fired upon, and wounded severely. He returned to the engine house, and fought bravely after that for fully an hour and a half, when he received a mortal wound, which he struggled under until the next day. The contemptible and savage manner in which the flag of truce had been received, induced severe measures in our defence, in the hour and a half before the next one was sent out. The effect of our work was, that the troops ceased to fire at the buildings, as we clearly had the advantage of position.

Capt. A. D. Stevens was next sent out with a flag, with what success I will presently show. Meantime, Jeremiah Anderson, who had brought the message from Kagi previously, was sent by Capt. Brown with another message to John Henrie, but before he got far on the street, he was fired upon and wounded. He returned at once to the engine house, where he survived but a short time. The ball, it was found, had entered the right side in such manner that death necessarily ensued speedily.

Capt. Stevens was fired upon several times while carrying his flag of truce, and received severe wounds, as I was informed that day, not being myself in a position to see him after. He was captured, and taken to the Wager House, where he was kept until the close of the struggle in the evening, when he was placed with the rest of our party who had been captured.

After the capture of Stevens, desperate fighting was done by both sides. The marines forced their way inside the engine-house yard, and commanded Capt. Brown to surrender, which he refused to do, but said in reply, that he was willing to fight them, if they would allow him first to withdraw his men to the second lock on the Maryland side. As might be expected, the cowardly hordes refused to entertain such a proposition, but continued their assault, to cut off communication between our several parties. The men at the Kennedy Farm having received such a favorable message in the early part of the day, through Thompson, were ignorant of the disastrous state of affairs later in the day. Could they have known the truth, and come down in time, the result would have been very different; we should not have been captured that day. A handful of determined men, as they were, by taking a position on the Maryland side, when the troops made their attack and retreated to the bridge for shelter, would have placed the enemy between two fires. Thompson's news prevented them from hurrying down, as they otherwise would have done, and thus deprived us of able assistance from Owen Brown, a host in himself, and Tidd, Merriam and Coppic, the brave fellows composing that band.

The climax of murderous assaults on that memorable day was the final capture of the engine house, with the old Captain and his handful of associates. This outrageous burlesque upon civilized warfare must have a special chapter to itself, as it concentrates more of Southern littleness and cowardice than is often believed to be true.

CHAPTER XIII.

THE CAPTURE OF CAPTAIN JOHN BROWN AT THE ENGINE HOUSE.

One great difference between savages and civilized nations is, the improved mode of warfare adopted by the latter. Flags of truce are always entitled to consideration, and an attacking party would make a wide departure from military usage, were they not to give opportunity for the besieged to capitulate, or to surrender at discretion. Looking at the Harper's Ferry combat in the light of civilized usage, even where one side might be regarded as insurrectionary, the brutal treatment of Captain Brown and his men in the charge by the marines on the engine house is deserving of severest condemnation, and is one of those blood-thirsty occurrences, dark enough in depravity to disgrace a century.

Captain Hazlett and myself being in the Arsenal opposite, saw the charge upon the engine house with the ladder, which resulted in opening the doors to the marines, and finally in Brown's capture. The old hero and his men were hacked and wounded with indecent rage, and at last brought out of the house and laid prostrate upon the ground, mangled and bleeding as they were. A formal surrender was required of Captain Brown, which he refused, knowing how little favor he would receive, if unarmed, at the hands of that infuriated mob. All of our party who went from the Farm, save the Captain, Shields Green, Edwin Coppic and Watson Brown, (who had received a mortal wound some time before,) the men at the Farm, and Hazlett and I, were either dead or captured before this time; the particulars of whose fate we learned still later in the day, as I shall presently show. Of the four prisoners taken at the engine house, Shields Green, the most inexorable of all our party, a very Turco in his hatred against the stealers of men, was under Captain Hazlett, and consequently of our little band at the Arsenal; but when we were ordered by Captain Brown to return to our positions, after having driven the troops into the bridge, he mistook the order, and went to the engine house instead of with his own party. Had he remained with us, he might have eluded the vigilant Virginians. As it was, he was doomed, as is well-known, and became a free-will offering for freedom, with his comrade, John Copeland. Wiser and better men no doubt there were, but a braver man never lived than Shields Green.

CHAPTER XIV.

SETTING FORTH REASONS WHY O. P. ANDERSON AND A. HAZLETT ESCAPED FROM THE ARSENAL, INSTEAD OF REMAINING, WHEN THEY HAD NOTHING TO DO—TOOK A PRISONER, AND WHAT RESULTED TO THEM, AND TO THIS NARRATIVE, THEREFROM—A PURSUIT, WHEN SOMEBODY GOT KILLED, AND OTHER BODIES WOUNDED.

Of the six men assigned a position in the arsenal by Captain Brown, four were either slain or captured; and Hazlett and myself, the only ones remaining, never left our position until we saw, with feelings of intense sadness, that we could be of no further avail to our commander, he being a prisoner in the hands of the Virginians. We therefore, upon consultation, concluded it was better to retreat while it was possible, as our work for the day was clearly finished, and gain a position where in the future we could work with better success, than to recklessly invite capture and brutality at the hands of our enemies. The charge of deserting our brave old leader and of fleeing from danger has been circulated to our detriment, but I have the consolation of knowing that, reckless as were the half-civilized hordes against whom we contended the entire day, and much as they might wish to disparage his men, they would never have thus charged us. They know better. John Brown's men at Harper's Ferry were and are a unit in their devotion to John Brown and the cause he espoused. To have deserted him would have been to belie every manly characteristic for which Albert Hazlett, at least, was known by the party to be distinguished, at the same time that it would have endangered the future safety of such deserter or deserters. John Brown gave orders; those orders must be obeyed, so long as Captain Brown was in a position to enforce them; once unable to command, from death, being a prisoner, or otherwise, the command devolved upon John Henry Kagi. Before Captain Brown was made prisoner, Captain Kagi had ceased to live, though had he been living, all communication between our post and him had been long cut off. We could not aid Captain Brown by remaining. We might, by joining the men at the Farm, devise plans for his succor; or our experience might become available on some future occasion.

The charge of running away from danger could only find form in the mind of some one unwilling to encounter the difficulties of a Harper's Ferry campaign, as no one acquainted with the out-of-door and in-door encounters of that day will charge any one with wishing to escape danger, merely. It is well enough for men out of danger, and who could not be induced to run the risk of a scratching, to talk flippantly about cowardice, and to sit in judgment upon the men who went with John Brown, and who did not fall into the hands of the Virginians; but to have been there, fought there, and to understand what *did* transpire there, are quite different. As Capt. Brown had all the prisoners with him, the whole force of the enemy was concentrated there, for a time, after the capture of the rifle factory. Having captured our commander, we knew that it was but little two of us could do against so many, and that our turn to be taken must come; so Hazlett and I went out at the back part of the building, climbed up the wall, and went upon the railway. Behind us, in the Arsenal, were thousands of dollars, we knew full well, but that wealth had no charms for us, and we hastened to communicate with the men sent to the Kennedy Farm. We travelled up the Shenandoah along the railroad, and overtook one of the citizens. He was armed, and had been in the fight in the afternoon. We took him prisoner, in order to facilitate our escape. He submitted without resistance, and quietly gave up his gun. From him, we learned substantially of the final struggle at the rifle factory, where the noble Kagi commanded. The number of citizens killed was, according to his opinion, much larger than either Hazlett or I had supposed, although we knew there were a great many killed and wounded together. He said there must be at least seventy killed, besides wounded. Hazlett had said there must be fifty, taking into account the defence of the three strong positions. I do not know positively, but would not put the figure below thirty killed, seeing many fall as I did, and knowing the "dead aim" principle upon which we defended ourselves. One of the Southern published accounts, it will be remembered, said twenty citizens were killed, another said fifteen. At last it got narrowed down to five, which was simply absurd, after so long an engagement. We had forty rounds apiece when we went to the Ferry, and when Hazlett and I left, we had not more than twenty rounds between us. The rest of the party were as free with their ammunition as we were, if not more so. We had further evidence that the number of dead was larger than published, from the many that we saw lying dead around.

When we had gone as far as the foot of the mountains, our prisoner begged us not to take his life, but to let him go at liberty. He said we might keep his gun; he would not inform on us. Feeling compassion for him, and trusting to his honor, we suffered him to go, when he went directly into town, and finding every thing there in the hands of our enemies, he informed on us, and we were pursued. After he had left us, we crawled or climbed up among the rocks in the mountains, some hundred yards or more from the spot where we left him, and hid ourselves, as we feared treachery, on second thought. A few minutes before dark, the troops came in search of us. They came to the foot of the mountains, marched and counter-marched, but never attempted to search the mountains; we supposed from their movements that they feared a host of armed enemies in concealment. Their air was so defiant, and their errand so distasteful to us, that we concluded to apply a little ammunition to their case, and having a few cartridges on hand, we poured from our excellent position in the rocky wilds, some well-directed shots. It was not so dark but that we could see one bite the dust now and then, when others would run to aid them instantly, particularly the wounded. Some lay where they fell, undisturbed, which satisfied us that they were dead. The troops returned our fire, but it was random shooting, as we were concealed from their sight by the rocks and bushes. Interchanging of shots continued for some minutes, with much spirit, when it became quite dark, and they went down into the town. After their return to the Ferry, we could hear the drum beating for a long time; an indication of their triumph, we supposed. Hazlett and I remained in our position three hours, before we dared venture down.

CHAPTER XV.

THE ENCOUNTER AT THE RIFLE FACTORY.

As stated in a previous chapter, the command of the rifle factory was given to Captain Kagi. Under him were John Copeland, Sherrard Lewis Leary, and three colored men from the neighborhood. At an early hour, Kagi saw from his position the danger in remaining, with our small company, until assistance could come to the inhabitants. Hence his suggestion to Captain Brown, through Jeremiah Anderson, to leave. His position being more isolated than the others, was the first to invite an organized attack with success; the Virginians first investing the factory with their hordes, before the final success at the engine house. From the prisoner taken by us who had participated in the assault upon Kagi's position, we received the sad details of the slaughter of our brave companions. Seven different times during the day they were fired upon, while they occupied the interior part of the building, the insurgents defending themselves with great courage, killing and wounding with fatal precision. At last, overwhelming numbers, as many as five hundred, our informant told us, blocked up the front of the building, battered the doors down, and forced their way into the interior. The insurgents were then forced to retreat the back way, fighting, however, all the time. They were pursued, when they took to the river, and it being so shallow, they waded out to a rock, mid-way, and there made a stand, being completely hemmed in, front and rear. Some four or five hundred shots, said our prisoner, were fired at them before they were conquered. They would not surrender into the hands of the enemy, but kept on fighting until every one was killed, except John Copeland. Seeing he could do no more, and that all his associates were murdered, he suffered himself to be captured. The party at the rifle factory fought desperately till the last, from their perch on the rock. Slave and free, black and white, carried out the special injunction of the brave old Captain, to make sure work of it. The unfortunate targets for so many bullets from the enemy, some of them received two or three balls. There fell poor Kagi, the friend and adviser of Captain Brown in his most trying positions, and the cleverest man in the party; and there also fell Sherrard Lewis Leary, generous-hearted and companionable as he was, and in that and other difficult positions, brave to desperation. There fought John Copeland, who met his fate like a man. But they were all "honorable men," noble, noble fellows, who fought and died for the most holy principles. John Copeland was taken to the guard-house, where the other prisoners afterwards were, and thence to Charlestown jail. His subsequent mockery of a trial, sentence and execution, with his companion Shields Green, on the 16th of December—are they not part of the dark deeds of this era, which will assign their perpetrators to infamy, and cause after generations to blush at the remembrance?

CHAPTER XVI.

OUR ESCAPE FROM VIRGINIA—HAZLETT BREAKS DOWN FROM FATIGUE AND HUNGER—NARROW ESCAPE IN PENNSYLVANIA.

I have said elsewhere, that Hazlett and I crossed over to the Maryland side, after the skirmish with the troops about nightfall. To be more circumstantial: when we descended from the rocks, we passed through the back part of the Ferry on the hill, down to the railroad, proceeding as far as the saw-mill on the Virginia side, where we came upon an old boat tied up to the shore, which we cast off, and crossed the Potomac. The Maryland shore once gained, we passed along the tow-path of the canal for some distance, when we came to an arch, which led through under the canal, and thence to the Kennedy Farm, hoping to find something to eat, and to meet the men who had been stationed on that side. When we reached the farm-house, all our expectations were disappointed. The old house had been ransacked and deserted, the provisions taken away, with every thing of value to the insurgents. Thinking that we should fare better at the school-house, we bent our steps in that direction. The night was dark and rainy, and after tramping for an hour and a half, at least, we came up to the school-house. This was about two o'clock in the morning. The school-house was packed with things moved there by the party the previous day, but we searched in vain, after lighting a match, for food, our great necessity, or for our young companions in the struggle. Thinking it unsafe to remain in the school-house, from fear of oversleeping ourselves, we climbed up the mountain in the rear of it, to lie down till daylight.

It was after sunrise some time when we awoke in the morning. The first sound we heard was shooting at the Ferry. Hazlett thought it must be Owen Brown and his men trying to force their way into the town, as they had been informed that a number of us had been taken prisoners, and we started down along the ridge to join them. When we got in sight of the Ferry, we saw the troops firing across the river to the Maryland side with considerable spirit. Looking closely, we saw, to our surprise, that they were firing upon a few of the colored men, who had been armed the day before by our men, at the Kennedy Farm, and stationed down at the school-house by C. P. Tidd. They were in the bushes on the edge of the mountains, dodging about, occasionally exposing themselves to the enemy. The troops crossed the bridge in pursuit of them, but they retreated in different directions. Being further in the mountains, and more secure, we could see without personal harm befalling us. One of the colored men came towards where we were, when we hailed him, and inquired the particulars. He said that one of his comrades had been shot, and was lying on the side of the mountains; that they thought the men who had armed them the day before must be in the Ferry. That opinion, we told him, was not correct. We asked him to join with us in hunting up the rest of the party, but he declined, and went his way.

While we were in this part of the mountains, some of the troops went to the school-house, and took possession of it. On our return along up the ridge, from our position, screened by the bushes, we could see them as they invested it. Our last hope of shelter, or of meeting our companions, now being destroyed, we concluded to make our escape North. We started at once, and wended our way along until dark, without being fortunate enough to overtake our friends, or to get any thing to eat. As may be supposed, from such incessant activity, and not having tasted a morsel for forty-eight hours, our appetites were exceedingly keen. So hungry were we, that we sought out a cornfield, under cover of the night, gathered some of the ears,—which, by the way, were pretty well hardened,—carried them into the mountains,—our fortunate resource,—and, having matches, struck fire, and roasted and feasted.

During our perilous and fatiguing journey to Pennsylvania, and for some time after crossing the line, our only food was corn roasted in the ear, often difficult to get without risk, and seldom eaten but at long intervals. As a result of this poor diet and the hard journey, we became nearly famished, and very much reduced in bodily strength. Poor Hazlett could not bear the privations as I could; he was less inured to physical exertion, and was of rather slight form, though inclined to be tall. With his feet blistered and sore, he held out as long as he could, but at last gave out, completely broken down, ten miles below Chambersburg. He declared it was impossible for him to go further, and begged me to go on, as we should be more in danger if seen together in the vicinity of the towns. He said, after resting that night, he would throw away his rifle, and go to Chambersburg in the stage next morning, where we agreed to meet again. The poor young man's face was wet with tears when we parted. I was loth to leave him, as we both knew that danger was more imminent than when in the mountains around Harper's Ferry. At the latter place, the ignorant slaveholding aristocracy were unacquainted with the topography of their own grand hills;—in Pennsylvania, the cupidity of the pro-slavery classes would induce them to seize a stranger on suspicion, or to go hunting for our party, so tempting to them is the bribe offered by the Slave Power. Their debasement in that respect was another reason why we felt the importance of travelling at night, as much as possible. After leaving young Hazlett, I travelled on as fast as my disabled condition would admit of, and got into Chambersburg about two hours after midnight.

I went cautiously, as I thought, to the house of an acquaintance, who arose and let me in. Before knocking, however, I hid my rifle a little distance from the house. My appearance caused my friend to become greatly agitated.

Having been suspected of complicity in the outbreak, although he was in ignorance of it until it happened, he was afraid that, should my whereabouts become known to the United States Marshal, he would get into serious difficulty. From him I learned that the Marshal was looking for Cook, and that it was not only unsafe for me to remain an hour, but that any one they chose to suspect would be arrested. I represented to him my famished condition, and told him I would leave as soon as I should be able to eat a morsel. After having despatched my hasty meal, and while I was busy filling my pockets with bread and meat, in the back part of the house, the United States Marshal knocked at the front door. I stepped out at the back door to be ready for flight, and while standing there, I heard the officer say to my friend, "You are suspected of harboring persons who were engaged in the Harper's Ferry outbreak." A warrant was then produced, and they said they must search the house. These Federal hounds were watching the house, and, supposing that who ever had entered was lying down, they expected to pounce upon their prey easily. Hearing what I did, I started quietly away to the place where I left my arms, gathered them up, and concluded to travel as far as I could before daylight. When morning came, I went off the road some distance to where there was a straw stack, where I remained throughout the day. At night, I set out and reached York, where a good Samaritan gave me oil, wine and raiment. From York, I wended my way to the Pennsylvania railroad. I took the train at night, at a convenient station, and went to Philadelphia, where great kindness was extended to me; and from there I came to Canada, without mishap or incident of importance. To avoid detection when making my escape, I was obliged to change my apparel three times, and my journey over the railway was at first in the night-time, I lying in concealment in the day-time.

CHAPTER XVII.

A WORD OR TWO MORE ABOUT ALBERT HAZLETT.

I left Lieut. Hazlett prostrate with fatigue and hunger, the night on which I went to Chambersburg. The next day, he went into the town boldly, carrying his blanket, rifle and revolver, and proceeded to the house where Kagi had boarded. The reward was then out for John E. Cook's arrest, and suspecting him to be Cook, Hazlett was pursued. He was chased from the house where he was by the officers, dropping his rifle in his flight. When he got to Carlisle, so far from receiving kindness from the citizens of his native State,—he was from Northern Pennsylvania,—he was arrested and lodged in jail, given up to the authorities of Virginia, and shamefully executed by them,—his identity, however, never having been proven before the Court. A report of his arrest at the time reads as follows:—

"The man arrested on suspicion of being concerned in the insurrection was brought before Judge Graham on a writ of *habeas corpus* to-day. Judge Watts presented a warrant from Governor Packer, of Pennsylvania, upon a requisition from the Governor of Virginia for the delivery of the fugitive named Albert Hazlett. There was no positive evidence to identify the prisoner."

Hazlett was remanded to the custody of the Sheriff. The Judge appointed a further hearing, and issued subpœnas for witnesses from Virginia, &c. No positive evidence in that last hearing was adduced, and yet Governor Packer ordered him to be delivered up; and the pro-slavery authorities made haste to carry out the mandate.

CHAPTER XVIII.

CAPT. OWEN BROWN, CHARLES P. TIDD, BARCLAY COPPIC, F. J. MERRIAM, JOHN E. COOK.

In order to have a proper understanding of the work done at Harper's Ferry, I will repeat, in a measure, separately, information concerning the movements of Capt. O. Brown and company, given in connection with other matter.

This portion of John Brown's men was sent to the Maryland side previous to the battle, except Charles P. Tidd and John E. Cook, who went with our party to the Ferry on Sunday evening. These two were of the company who took Col. Washington prisoner, but on Monday morning, they were ordered to the Kennedy Farm, to assist in moving and guarding arms. Having heard, through some means, that the conflict was against the insurgents, they provided themselves with food, blankets, and other necessaries, and then took to the mountains. They were fourteen days making the journey to Chambersburg. The weather was extremely bad the whole time; it rained, snowed, blew, and was freezing cold; but there was no shelter for the fugitive travellers, one of whom, F. J. Merriam, was in poor health, lame, and physically slightly formed. He was, however, greatly relieved by his companions, who did every thing possible to lessen the fatigue of the journey for him. The bad weather, and their destitution, made it one of the most trying journeys it is possible for men to perform. Sometimes they would have to lie over a day or two for the sick, and when fording streams, as they had to do, they carried the sick over on their shoulders.

They were a brave band, and any attempt to arrest them in a body would have been a most serious undertaking, as all were well armed, could have fired some forty rounds apiece, and would have done it, without any doubt whatever. The success of the Federal officers consisted in arresting those unfortunate enough to fall into their clutches singly. In this manner did poor Hazlett and John E. Cook fall into their power.

Starvation several times stared Owen Brown's party in the face. They would search their pockets over and over for some stray crumb that might have been overlooked in the general search, for something to appease their gnawing hunger, and pick out carefully, from among the accumulated dirt and medley, even the smallest crumb, and give it to the comrade least able to endure the long and biting fast.

John E. Cook became completely overcome by this hungry feeling. A strong desire to get salt pork took possession of him, and against the remonstrances of his comrades, he ventured down from the mountains to Montaldo, a settlement fourteen miles from Chambersburg, in quest of it. He was arrested by Daniel Logan and Clegget Fitzhugh, and taken before Justice Reisher. Upon examination, a commission signed by Captain Brown, marked No. 4, being found upon his person, he was committed to await a requisition from Governor Wise, and finally, as is well-known, was surrendered to Virginia, where he was tried, after a fashion, condemned, and executed. It is not my intention to dwell upon the failings of John E. Cook. That he departed from the record, as familiar to John Brown and his men, every one of them "posted" in the details of their obligations and duties, well-knows; but his very weakness should excite our compassion. He was brave—none could doubt that, and life was invested with charms for him, which his new relation as a man of family tended to intensify; and charity suggests that the hope of escaping his merciless persecutors, and of being spared to his friends and associates in reform, rather than treachery to the cause he had espoused, furnishes the explanation of his peculiar sayings.

Owen Brown, and the other members of the party, becoming impatient at Cook's prolonged absence, began to suspect something was wrong, and moved at once to a more retired and safer position. Afterwards, they went to Chambersburg, and stopped in the outskirts of the town for some days, communicating with but one person, directly, while there. Through revelations made by Cook, it became unsafe in the neighborhood, and they left, and went some miles from town, when Merriam took the cars for Philadelphia; thence to Boston, and subsequently to Canada. The other three travelled on foot to Centre County, Pennsylvania, when Barclay Coppic separated from them, to take the cars, with the rifles of the company boxed up in his possession. He stopped at Salem, Ohio, a few days, and then went to Cleveland; from Cleveland to Detroit, and over into Canada, where, after remaining for a time, he proceeded westward. Owen Brown and C. P. Tidd went to Ohio, where the former spent the winter. The latter, after a sojourn, proceeded to Massachusetts.

CHAPTER XIX.

THE BEHAVIOR OF THE SLAVES—CAPTAIN BROWN'S OPINION.

Of the various contradictory reports made by slaveholders and their satellites about the time of the Harper's Ferry conflict, none were more untruthful than those relating to the slaves. There was seemingly a studied attempt to enforce the belief that the slaves were cowardly, and that they were really more in favor of Virginia masters and slavery, than of their freedom. As a party who had an intimate knowledge of the conduct of the colored men engaged, I am prepared to make an emphatic denial of the gross imputation against them. They were charged specially with being unreliable, with deserting Captain Brown the first opportunity, and going back to their masters; and with being so indifferent to the work of their salvation from the yoke, as to have to be forced into service by the Captain, contrary to their will.

On the Sunday evening of the outbreak, when we visited the plantations and acquainted the slaves with our purpose to effect their liberation, the greatest enthusiasm was manifested by them—joy and hilarity beamed from every countenance. One old mother, white-haired from age, and borne down with the labors of many years in bonds, when told of the work in hand, replied: "God bless you! God bless you!" She then kissed the party at her house, and requested all to kneel, which we did, and she offered prayer to God for His blessing on the enterprise, and our success. At the slaves' quarters, there was apparently a general jubilee, and they stepped forward manfully, without impressing or coaxing. In one case, only, was there any hesitation. A dark-complexioned free-born man refused to take up arms. He showed the only want of confidence in the movement, and far less courage than any slave consulted about the plan. In fact, so far as I could learn, the free blacks South are much less reliable than the slaves, and infinitely more fearful. In Washington City, a party of free colored persons offered their services to the Mayor, to aid in suppressing our movement. Of the slaves who followed us to the Ferry, some were sent to help remove stores, and the others were drawn up in a circle around the engine-house, at one time, where they were, by Captain Brown's order, furnished by me with pikes, mostly, and acted as a guard to the prisoners to prevent their escape, which they did.

As in the war of the American Revolution, the first blood shed was a black man's, Crispus Attuck's, so at Harper's Ferry, the first blood shed by our party, after the arrival of the United States troops, was that of a slave. In the beginning of the encounter; and before the troops had fairly emerged from the bridge, a slave was shot. I saw him fall. Phil, the slave who died in prison, with fear, as it was reported, was wounded at the Ferry, and died from the effects of it. Of the men shot on the rocks, when Kagi's party were compelled to take to the river, some were slaves, and they suffered death before they would desert their companions, and their bodies fell into the waves beneath. Captain Brown, who was surprised and pleased by the promptitude with which they volunteered, and with their manly bearing at the scene of violence, remarked to me, on that Monday morning, that he was agreeably disappointed in the behavior of the slaves; for he did not expect one out of ten to be willing to fight. The truth of the Harper's Ferry "raid," as it has been called, in regard to the part taken by the slaves, and the aid given by colored men generally, demonstrates clearly: First, that the conduct of the slaves is a strong guarantee of the weakness of the institution, should a favorable opportunity occur; and, secondly, that the colored people, as a body, were well represented by numbers, both in the fight, and in the number who suffered martyrdom afterward.

The first report of the number of "insurrectionists" killed was *seventeen*, which showed that several slaves were killed; for there were only *ten* of the men that belonged to the Kennedy Farm who lost their lives at the Ferry, namely: John Henri Kagi, Jerry Anderson, Watson Brown, Oliver Brown, Stewart Taylor, Adolphus Thompson, William Thompson, William Leeman, all eight whites, and Dangerfield Newby and Sherrard Lewis Leary, both colored. The rest reported dead, according to their own showing, were colored. Captain Brown had but seventeen with him, belonging to the Farm, and when all was over, there were four besides himself taken to Charlestown, prisoners, viz: A. D. Stevens, Edwin Coppic, white; John A. Copeland and Shields Green, colored. It is plain to be seen from this, that there was a proper per centage of colored men killed at the Ferry, and executed at Charlestown. Of those that escaped from the fangs of the human bloodhounds of slavery, there were four whites, and one colored man, myself being the sole colored man of those at the Farm.

That hundreds of slaves were ready, and would have joined in the work, had Captain Brown's sympathies not been aroused in favor of the families of his prisoners, and that a very different result would have been seen, in consequence, there is no question. There was abundant opportunity for him and the party to leave a place in which they held entire sway and possession, before the arrival of the troops. And so cowardly were the slaveholders, proper, that from Colonel Lewis Washington, the descendant of the Father of his Country, General George Washington, they were easily taken prisoners. They had not pluck enough to fight, nor to use the well-loaded arms in their possession, but were concerned rather in keeping a whole skin by parleying, or in spilling cowardly tears, to excite pity, as did Colonel

Washington, and in that way escape merited punishment. No, the conduct of the slaves was beyond all praise; and could our brave old Captain have steeled his heart against the entreaties of his captives, or shut up the fountain of his sympathies against their families—could he, for the moment, have forgotten them, in the selfish thought of his own friends and kindred, or, by adhering to the original plan, have left the place, and thus looked forward to the prospective freedom of the slave—hundreds ready and waiting would have been armed before twenty-four hours had elapsed. As it was, even the noble old man's mistakes were productive of great good, the fact of which the future historian will record, without the embarrassment attending its present narration. John Brown did not only capture and hold Harper's Ferry for twenty hours, but he held the whole South. He captured President Buchanan and his Cabinet, convulsed the whole country, killed Governor Wise, and dug the mine and laid the train which will eventually dissolve the union between Freedom and Slavery. The rebound reveals the truth. So let it be!

[From the New York Tribune.]

HOW OLD JOHN BROWN TOOK HARPER'S FERRY.

A BALLAD FOR THE TIMES.

[*Containing ye True History of ye Great Virginia Fright.*]

John Brown in Kansas settled, like a steadfast Yankee farmer,

Brave and godly, with four sons—all stalwart men of might;

There he spoke aloud for Freedom, and the Border-strife grew warmer,

Till the Rangers fired his dwelling, in his absence in the night—

And Old Brown,

Osawatomie Brown,

Came homeward in the morning, to find his house burned down.

Then he grasped his trusty rifle, and boldly fought for Freedom;

Smote from border unto border the fierce invading band;

And he and his brave boys vowed—so might Heaven help and speed 'em!—

They would save those grand old prairies from the curse that blights the
land;

And Old Brown,

Osawatomie Brown,

Said—"Boys, the Lord will aid us!" and he shoved his ramrod down.

And the Lord *did* aid these men, and they labored day and even,

Saving Kansas from its peril—and their very lives seemed charmed;

Till the Ruffians killed one son, in the blesséd light of heaven—

In cold blood the fellows slew him, as he journeyed all unarmed;

Then Old Brown,

Osawatomie Brown,

Shed not a tear, but shut his teeth, and frowned a terrible frown.

Then they seized another brave boy—not amid the heat of battle,

But in peace, behind his plough-share—and they loaded him with chains,

And with pikes, before their horses, even as they goad their cattle,

Drove him, cruelly, for their sport, and at last blew out his brains;

Then Old Brown,

Osawatomie Brown,

Raised his right hand up to Heaven, calling Heaven's vengeance down.

And he swore a fearful oath, by the name of the Almighty,

He would hunt this ravening evil, that had scathed and torn him so—

He would seize it by the vitals; he would crush it day and night: he

Would so pursue its footsteps—so return it blow for blow—

That Old Brown,

Osawatomie Brown,

Should be a name to swear by, in backwoods or in town!

Then his beard became more grizzled, and his wild blue eye grew wilder,

And more sharply curved his hawk's nose, snuffing battle from afar;

And he and the two boys left, though the Kansas strife waxed milder,

Grew more sullen, till was over the bloody Border War,

And Old Brown,

Osawatomie Brown,

Had grown crazy, as they reckoned, by his fearful glare and frown.

So he left the plains of Kansas and their bitter woes behind him—

Slipt off into Virginia, where the statesmen all are born—

Hired a farm by Harper's Ferry, and no one knew where to find him,

Or whether he had turned parson, and was jacketed and shorn,

For Old Brown,

Osawatomie Brown,

Mad as he was, knew texts enough to wear a parson's gown.

He bought no ploughs and harrows, spades and shovels, or such trifles,

But quietly to his rancho there came, by every train,

Boxes full of pikes and pistols, and his well-beloved Sharp's rifles;

And eighteen other madmen joined their leader there again.

Says Old Brown,

Osawatomie Brown,

"Boys, we have got an army large enough to whip the town!

"Whip the town and seize the muskets, free the negroes, and then arm
them—

Carry the County and the State; ay, and all the potent South;

On their own heads be the slaughter, if their victims rise to harm them—

These Virginians! who believed not, nor would heed the warning mouth."

Says Old Brown,

Osawatomie Brown,

"The world shall see a Republic, or my name is not JOHN BROWN!"

'Twas the sixteenth of October, on the evening of a Sunday—
"This good work," declared the Captain, "shall be on a holy night!"
It was on a Sunday evening, and before the noon of Monday,
With two sons, and Captain Stevens, fifteen privates—black and white—

Captain Brown,
Osawatomie Brown,
Marched across the bridged Potomac, and knocked the sentinel down;

Took the guarded armory building, and the muskets and the cannon;
Captured all the country majors and the colonels, one by one;
Scared to death each gallant scion of Virginia they ran on,
And before the noon of Monday, I say, the deed was done.
Mad Old Brown,
Osawatomie Brown,
With his eighteen other crazy men, went in and took the town.

Very little noise and bluster, little smell of powder, made he;
It was all done in the midnight, like the Emperor's *coup d'etat*:
"Cut the wires: stop the rail-cars: hold the streets and bridges!" said he—
Then declared the new Republic, with himself for guiding star—
This Old Brown,
Osawatomie Brown!
And the bold two thousand citizens ran off and left the town.

Then was riding and railroading and expressing here and thither!
And the MARTINSBURG SHARPSHOOTERS, and the CHARLESTOWN
VOLUNTEERS,
And the SHEPHERDSTOWN and WINCHESTER MILITIA hastened whither
Old Brown was said to muster his ten thousand grenadiers!
General Brown,
Osawatomie Brown!

Behind whose rampant banner all the North was pouring down.

But at last, 'tis said, some prisoners escaped from Old Brown's durance,
And the effervescent valor of Ye Chivalry broke forth,

When they learned that nineteen madmen had the marvellous assurance—
Only nineteen—thus to seize the place, and drive them frightened forth;
And Old Brown,
Osawatomie Brown,
Found an army come to take him encamped around the town.

But to storm with all the forces we have mentioned was too risky;
So they hurried off to Richmond for the GOVERNMENT MARINES—
Tore them from their weeping matrons—fired their souls with Bourbon whiskey—
Till they battered down Brown's castle with their ladders and machines;
And Old Brown,
Osawatomie Brown,
Received three bayonet stabs, and a cut on his brave old crown.

Tallyho! the old Virginia gentry gathered to the baying!
In they rush and kill the game, shooting lustily away![A]
And whene'er they slay a rebel, those who come too late for slaying,
Not to lose a share of glory, fire their bullets in his clay;
And Old Brown,
Osawatomie Brown,
Saw his sons fall dead beside him, and between them laid him down.

How the conquerors wore their laurels—how they hastened on the trials—
How Old Brown was placed, half-dying, on the Charlestown Court-House floor—

How he spoke his grand oration, in the scorn of all denials—

What the brave old madman told them—these are known the country o'er.

"Hang Old Brown,

Osawatomie Brown,"

Said the Judge, "and all such rebels!" with his most judicial frown.

But, Virginians, don't do it! for I tell you that the flagon,

Filled with blood of Old Brown's offspring, was first poured by Southern hands:

And each drop from Old Brown's life-veins, like the red gore of the dragon,

May spring up a vengeful Fury, hissing through your slave-worn lands;

And Old Brown,

Osawatomie Brown,

May trouble you more than ever, when you've nailed his coffin down!

FOOTNOTES:

[A] "The hunt was up—woe to the game enclosed within that fiery circle! The town was occupied by a thousand or fifteen hundred men, including volunteer companies from Shepherdstown, Charlestown, Winchester, and elsewhere; but the armed and unorganized multitude largely predominated, giving the affair more the character of a great hunting scene than that of a battle. The savage game was holed beyond all possibility of escape."—*Virginia Correspondent of Harper's Weekly.*

[From the Boston Liberator.]
JOHN BROWN OF OSAWATOMIE.
BY G. D. WHITMORE.

So you've convicted old John Brown! brave old Brown of Osawatomie!

And you gave him a *chivalrous* trial, lying groaning on the floor,

With his body ripped with gashes, deaf with pain from sabre slashes,

Over the head received, when the deadly fight was o'er;

Round him guns with lighted matches, judge and lawyers pale as ashes—

For he might, perhaps, come to again, and put you all to flight,

Or surround you, as before!

You think, no doubt, *you*'ve tried John Brown, but he's laid there trying *you*,
And the world has been his jury, and its judgment's swift and true:
Over the globe the tale has rung, back to your hearts the verdict's flung,
That you're found, as you've been always found, a brutal, cowardly crew!
At the wave of his hand to a dozen men, two thousand slunk like hounds;
He kennelled you up, and kept you too, till twice you saw through the azure blue,
The day-star circle round.

No longer the taunt, our history's new, "our hero is yet to come"—
We've suddenly leaped a thousand years beyond the rolling sun!
And, sheeted round with a martyr's glory, again on earth's renewed the story
Of bravery, truth, and righteousness, a battle lost and won;
A life laid down for the poor and weak, the immortal crown put on;
The spark of Luther's touched to the pile—swords gleam—black smoke obscures the sun—
And the slave and his master are gone!

Ages hence, when all is over that shocks the sense of the world to-day,
Pilgrims will mount the western wave, seeking the new Thermopylæ;
Then, for that brave old man with many sons, mangled and murdered, one by one,
Whose ghosts rise up from Harper's gorge, Missouri's plains, and far away
Where Kansas' grains wave tinged with their blood, will the column rise!
The Poet's song and History's page will the deeds prolong of John of Osawatomie,
The Martyr to Truth and Right!

[From the New York Independent.]
THE VIRGINIA SCAFFOLD.

Rear on high the scaffold altar! all the world will turn to see
How a man has dared to suffer that his brothers may be free!
Hear it on some hill-side looking North and South and East and West,
Where the wind from every quarter fresh may blow upon his breast,
And the sun look down unshaded from the chill December sky,
Glad to shine upon the hero who for Freedom dared to die!

All the world will turn to see him;—from the pines of wave-washed Maine
To the golden rivers rolling over California's plain,
And from clear Superior's waters, where the wild swan loves to sail,
To the Gulf-lands, summer-bosomed, fanned by ocean's softest gale,—
Every heart will beat the faster in its sorrow or its scorn,
For the man nor courts nor prisons can annoy another morn!
And from distant climes and nations men shall westward gaze, and say,
"He who perilled all for Freedom on the scaffold dies to-day."

Never offering was richer, nor did temple fairer rise
For the gods serenely smiling from the blue Olympian skies;
Porphyry or granite column did not statelier cleave the air
Than the posts of yonder gallows with the cross-beam waiting there;
And the victim, wreathed and crownéd, not for Dian nor for Jove,
But for Liberty and Manhood, comes, the sacrifice of Love.

They may hang him on the gibbet; they may raise the victor's cry,
When they see him darkly swinging like a speck against the sky;—
Ah! the dying of a hero, that the right may win its way,
Is but sowing seed for harvest in a warm and mellow May!

Now his story shall be whispered by the firelight's evening glow,

And in fields of rice and cotton, when the hot noon passes slow,
Till his name shall be a watch-word from Missouri to the sea,
And his planting find its reaping in the birthday of the Free!

Christ, the crucified, attend him, weak and erring though he be;
In his measure he has striven, suffering Lord! to love like Thee;
Thou the vine—thy friends the branches—is he not a branch of Thine,
Though some dregs from earthly vintage have defiled the heavenly wine?
Now his tendrils lie unclaspéd, bruised and prostrate on the sod,—
Take him to thine upper garden, where the husbandman is God!

"OLD JOHN BROWN."
BY REV. E. H. SEARS.

Not any spot six feet by two
Will hold a man like thee;
John Brown will tramp the shaking earth,
From Blue Ridge to the sea,
Till the strong angel comes at last,
And opes each dungeon door,
And God's "Great Charter" holds and waves
O'er all his humble poor.

And then the humble poor will come,
In that far-distant day,
And from the felon's nameless grave
They'll brush the leaves away;
And gray old men will point the spot
Beneath the pine-tree shade,
As children ask with streaming eyes
Where "Old John Brown" is laid.

DIRGE

Sung at a Meeting in Concord, Mass., Dec. 2, 1859.

To-day, beside Potomac's wave,
Beneath Virginia's sky,
They slay the man who loved the slave,
And dared for him to die.

The Pilgrim Fathers' earnest creed,
Virginia's ancient faith,
Inspired this hero's noblest deed,
And his reward is—Death!

Great Washington's indignant shade
For ever urged him on—
He heard from Monticello's glade
The voice of Jefferson.

But chiefly on the Hebrew page
He read Jehovah's law,
And this from youth to hoary age
Obeyed with love and awe.

No selfish purpose armed his hand,
No passion aimed his blow;
How loyally he loved his land,
Impartial Time shall show.

But now the faithful martyr dies,
His brave heart beats no more,
His soul ascends the equal skies,

His earthly course is o'er.

For this we mourn, but not for him,—
Like him in God we trust;
And though our eyes with tears are dim,
We know that God is just.

www.ingramcontent.com/pod-product-compliance
Ingram Content Group UK Ltd.
Pitfield, Milton Keynes, MK11 3LW, UK
UKHW020048311224
452994UK00004B/400